Cora the Cat
On Loan from God

Barbara Morris

Print ISBN: 978-1-958890-29-5
Ebook ISBN: 979-8-88531-283-7

Published by BookLocker.com, Inc., Trenton, Georgia, U.S.A.

Printed on acid-free paper.

Library of Congress Cataloguing in Publication Data
Morris, Barbara
Cora the Cat: On Loan from God by Barbara Morris
Library of Congress Control Number: 2023911487

BookLocker.com, Inc.
2023

Dedication

With love to Ward, my cat-loving
husband of fifty-six years

and

Cora, the sweet rescue cat who healed my heart.

Cora the cat

Adapting warily

To what life offers.

Barbara Morris

Introduction

My cat, Cora, was the best cat in the world. You may debate me on that, but after you hear her story, you will see why. She was not only the sweetest, cutest, most loveable, and well behaved (when it suited her) cat, but she was also the most intelligent cat you've ever met. At the same time, she had—let's just say—her limitations . . . You see, Cora was deaf. She was a thirteen-year-old rescue cat who had a God-given purpose in life. This purpose was to comfort me after my husband suddenly died. Let me tell you: Cora worked hard to fulfill this assignment. Like all cats, she worked hard to be sweet, adorable, and comforting. This meant she purred when petted, got underfoot at dinnertime, she head-butted for attention, slept a lot, sprawled in the sun with a smile on her face, curled on my lap *when she felt like it,* and tucked her head into the crook of my elbow *when she felt like it.* And when she did feel like it, the comfort she gave was heaven for both of us.

I wasn't the only one who needed comfort. It turns out Cora also needed attention. Her beloved owner, Marjorie, had just died. Cora desperately needed a "forever home" and loving care, which I had in abundance. So, with God's wisdom, Cora and I became helpmates for a year-and-a-half.

Cora and I spent a beautiful eighteen months together during which Cora, sadly, developed severe dementia and had to be euthanized. However, even in that confused state, she truly was God's life-reviving gift to me, which I knew from the moment she came into my life. I felt so strongly about it that I wanted to shout it to the world. This book is my shout.

Once I decided to write this book, I realized that I needed help—lots of it. My professional writing, for the most part, was humor or travel related. What I needed now was advice about how to tell the story of my relationship with Cora—something very dear to my heart. So, I joined Cora in a sunny corner where she was drowsing.

"Any ideas of what to write about us?" I asked Cora.

The sideways look she tossed me said it all: "Easy. You love me. I love you. But right now, I'm tired. Go write your book and let me sleep," she yawned. She was no help at all, but her yawn was contagious. I slumped down in the sunny corner next to her and napped.

About an hour later, I awakened with a start when, clearly, in my brain, I heard the first sentence of the book. I sprang up. My ninety-year-old "springing" took a minute or two while I massaged my achy knees and grasped the arm of my chair in a death grip. This was not the time to fall and break a hip. I had a book to write.

That afternoon as I slept the first sentence of this book that came to me is on the next page…

Chapter 1

On September 21, 2021, God gave me a special gift: Cora, the cat. I understood this gift right away. My husband had suddenly died, and the way I see it, God put Cora in my life to comfort me. You might think when God gives you something really special, it would be beautifully wrapped with a big heavenly bow, but this was not the case with Cora. God must have run out of wrapping paper because Cora came unwrapped and was in disarray. In fact, when I received her, she was the messiest ball of unkempt, dull, matted fur. She was such a frightened and huddled cat! Some gift, right?

Despite her appearance, God in His wisdom had sent another gift along with Cora—the gift of love. He sent it in big, billowing heaps so that the moment Cora was in my home, I loved her with the kind of love that hits you so hard, you think you've been pounded by a tsunami.

When I first tried to pet Cora, she (of course) hissed, spit, stiffened her spine, and bit me. She then took refuge under the table. Obviously, it didn't feel like the storybook beginning of a loving relationship. However, I empathized with her. I cooed to Cora that I knew she felt threatened, scared, and alone. I had to get down on my ninety-year-old hands and knees and crawl under the end table to tell her. I did what it took because Cora, slit-eyed, wary, and pathetic, was, like me, about 95% deaf.

What do you suppose God was thinking when He decided that Cora and I would make a team? Did He look at us, slump-shouldered, bleary-eyed and both of us having recently lost our best friends? Cora's devoted owner, Marjorie, had just passed away; Ward, my dear husband of fifty-six years had passed away too. Did God look with sympathy at me when I howl-sobbed into Ward's pillow? Did He want to pick up and cuddle Cora when she scrunched herself into a shabby ball in a dark back closet? Did He cradle His chin in his hands, nod sagely and, in heavenly tones, murmur, "The perfect pair! Boy, do they need one another!"

God knew what he was doing, of course. You see, Cora and I had so much in common. For one, in human years both of us are in our nineties. And then there's our deafness. I incline my head and say "Huh?" a lot; Cora just cocks her head and looks puzzled. God was also aware, naturally, that both of us are on meds for high blood pressure and lurking kidney problems; our arthritic bodies ache, and it takes both of us forever to ease our groaning joints into a comfortable position. So, yes: we are two peas in a pod.

It is so uncanny. As I write this, I'm seeing almost for the first time what bad shape both Cora and I were in. Isn't it amazing that in the vast expanse of the universe, God took the time to consider the deep, personal needs of two of his children? You see, I believe that Cora, too, is a child of God. The fact that God reached out to each of us, one-on-one, is beyond incredible. Beyond human words. Even I, a professional writer, can't describe this. When I try to imagine God turning his eye on me, instinctively I lower my head, my breath stops and, incredibly, I feel . . . I feel shy. But perhaps little Cora, dozing in the sun now with one paw curled over her eye, has the right response: she simply accepts that God has taken her in hand—that she's loved; that she's comfy with a full tummy—and that's that.

This is the story of how we two, both God's creatures, have been given the challenge of caring for and loving one another. Cora and I loving each other was our mutual purpose—our communal prayer to God. I have tried to explain all this to Cora, but she was singularly uninterested. She was waiting impatiently for din-din. (Okay, I admit it. Like millions of cat owners, I baby-talk to Cora at times, and din-din is one of the silliest words.) As you read our story, however, I think you'll see why Cora and I needed one another, why our companionship is "the best of prayers to God," and why Cora and I go together as naturally as gin and tonic or peanut butter and jelly.

God, in His wisdom, didn't just plop a cat on a complete cat-novice. Before I was married, I was a novice about both cats and dogs. In fact, I was a novice about any pet. It's not that I didn't try, however. At age ten I spent my allowance on a sweet little goldfish named Oscar, but in a rush of love, I over-fed him. I learned the sad lesson that sometimes you can have too much of a good thing. In His loving concern for Cora, God gave her to someone who eventually became a devoted cat person. That person is me! I and my late husband—a true cat lover—devoted ourselves to seven cats over thirty-five years. Thus, I'd like to tell you a little about these delightful pets who preceded Cora and who prepared her path to me. The next chapters will be devoted to that.

Before I tell you about the wonderful cats that came before Cora, I must mention again that sadly almost two years after God introduced Cora and me, He lovingly called Cora back to Him. She had been on loan. Her work, to reawaken my dispirited soul and to bring purpose to my life, was done. Only part of my assignment was complete: to restore Cora's unkempt little body, and, more importantly, to fill her life with trust, security, and love. The rest of my assignment was to use my God-given talent to write about the remarkable heavenly relationship between Cora and me. Moreover, our story is a tribute to God's special gift to me.

And now, to all the precious cats who paved Cora's way to my heart and home . . .

Chapter 2

My first cat charged into my life fifty-eight years ago. It was not a joyous occasion. The cat was a cantankerous Siamese who hated me at first sight. We met in Germany when my husband, Ward, came home one day with an armload of mean-eyed, tough-talkin' cat who took one look at me and glared a warning not to come one inch closer. I suspect he sensed I didn't know anything about cats—and that perhaps I didn't especially care for them.

We were in the bleak seaport of Bremerhaven because Ward, a Navy Lieutenant, had been ordered there a month after our marriage. We lived in a grim row of concrete government apartment buildings, each with a small, bare, iron-barred balcony. As Ward carried the cat in his arms, I recognized the cat immediately. The whole neighborhood knew the cat because he sat on his balcony about twelve hours every day, rain, or shine, while his owners were at work. We all called him The Balcony Cat.

Let me tell you—this cat was pathetic. Even I felt a pang of sympathy for him now and then. And now, here he was in our apartment because my husband—a cat lover, it turns out—had offered to cat sit for a week while his owners were on vacation. It was a week of learning, of give and take, of God gently nudging each of us toward one another physically and emotionally.

My pangs of sympathy burst into full bloom when Ward told me that The Balcony Cat didn't have a name. "They haven't thought of one yet," he said. For me that was a gut punch. To own a pet and not care about it enough to even give it a name! My scowl softened as I glanced at the Siamese who, now, was sensuously winding his body around Ward's legs and looking up at Ward with a look of adoration worthy of the shepherds and wise men.

I have no idea why I suddenly blurted, "Let's call him Max." A divine inspiration, perhaps? Whatever it was that inspired me, it gave me my first small connection with The Balcony Cat. If you give someone or something a name, you've invested a bit of yourself in that creature.

Max and I danced back and forth, physically, and emotionally, all week. I smiled at him; he only scratched me once. I called to him lovingly; he came to within a foot of me, leaned slightly toward me and almost looked as if he wanted to be petted. I gave him a quick scratch between his ears; he lowered his head and butted my hand. By the end of the week, I was stroking under his chin, and he was inviting me to pet his tummy.

Ward and I held one another close and cried the day Ward took Max back to his balcony. It was our first shared sorrow—and our first shared prayer that Max's life would improve. Often, throughout our fifty-six years of marriage and sharing our love with seven cats, Ward and I remembered sweet, dear, needy Max and were grateful that God had given us the opportunity and responsibility of bringing a bit of comfort and love into his life—if only for one precious week…

Chapter 3

Early on, Ward and I agreed that parenting wasn't in our DNA, so we decided not to have kids of our own. That does not mean, however, we did not enjoy borrowing our friends' kids for the day. We loved to challenge them to new adventures, scream with them on Roller Coasters, snorkel in Hawaii, share our love of ballets, symphonies, and drama. At day's end, we'd return the tired, grubby, sticky, and cranky kids to their parents.

We loved it, but as I look back on what happened, I suspect God was hatching plans for us to enjoy and accept more meaningful activities—more than just fun-for-a-day. I realize now, in spite of the good times, we were missing something deeper. We were missing the heartfelt connections, the understanding and unselfish love that comes from lives united by caring and being responsible to one another. I'm sure God thought Ward and I were ready for fuller lives by taking on the Christian challenge of helping others in need. I can practically hear Him warning us, "Okay, guys, time for a serious dive. Take a deep breath." And then it happened . . .

Petrouchka, a seal-point Siamese, pranced into our lives while we were in Germany. Her nickname was Trushkie, and she was the first of seven wonderful cats who shared our lives and love over the next forty-five years. In fact, she was the first of eight cats I have had the pleasure of caring for.

Petrouchka was born happy—and beautiful. Her fur was pale ivory with a dusting of mocha on her ears, paws, and tail. Total elegance. That bright little cat looked smashing—and she knew it; she strutted her stuff. When I said she pranced, I meant it literally. Moreover, Trushkie seemed game for anything.

Adventure? Bring it on! Trushkie enjoyed going for a drive in our VW, perched on Ward's shoulder as he drove so more pedestrians could see her and admire her there. Her vanity reached its height when we slipped a bright red leash around her neck so she could stroll with us as we toured Germany. After some initial tension ("What's this thing they've slapped on me?") I believe Trushkie realized the bright red color against her ivory fur was gorgeous. Her prancing took on a jaunty air delighting the animal loving Germans who fawned over her when we walked in the park.

But for all of her *très chic* appearances, at heart Trushkie was fun-loving and playful. For example, one weekend we took her to a German Inn. In a playful moment Ward picked her up and gently tossed her onto the cloud-like down quilt at the end of the bed. Instantly she disappeared down, down, down into the soft depths of the billowy quilt. Then, instantly, she clambered up and popped into view—her eyes alight with boundless joy. More! And so began the game of "Toss Trushkie," which went on for a full hour thanks to Trushkie's endless energy. When we tried to stop, she screamed, as only a Siamese can do, for more. Although our arms were weary, Ward and I kept laughing while tossing Trushkie and tumbling in the quilt with her. We had never seen such a happy cat.

I will be forever grateful for that wonderful evening because five days later we lost that sweet cat. Although spaying is a simple operation, Trushkie died on the operating table while being spayed. Despite knowing that spaying was routine, Ward and I were frightened and worried at the thought of Trushkie being anesthetized. Before leaving for work that morning, instead of his usual farewell pat on Trushkie's rump, Ward picked her up to rub noses and whisper goodbye. When I left her at the vet's, huddled and whimpering, I kissed her goodbye on the forehead. After that, I went home to await the call to pick her up later in the day. Instead of bringing her home when the call came, I learned she had succumbed to the anesthesia. Breathless with shock, I gave permission to cremate our dear little girl.

Ward and I spent the day and long into the night clinging to one another, sobbing, wailing, crying out we didn't understand. God wasn't a major part of our life in those days. Back then, we were Easter and Christmas church-going Christians, so we were too heartsick and angry to think of asking Him for comfort. Instead, with great determination, we set out to find another Siamese to fill our empty hearts…

Chapter 4

At this point in our lives, we were still stationed in Germany. Ward and I hadn't thought much about God, but He hadn't taken His eye off us. He had watched our love for one another deepen as we adored and cared for Trushkie. And, although Ward and I didn't know it, looking back, I'm sure God also had a practical purpose in mind. He knew what Ward had said to me even before we were married: "Because I'm in Naval Intelligence, my job is secret. I can never talk to you about work, even casual stuff, for fear of inadvertently disclosing something I shouldn't." And so, after we lost Trushkie, God very definitely gave us something to talk about; He gave us two robust, male Siamese kittens to raise, learn from, make parenting mistakes on, laugh at, worry about, and most of all, love with all our heart and soul.

The first to arrive was a chocolate brown ball of fur whom Ward immediately named Donner—after the God of Thunder because, despite his size, he seemed strong and manly, well-developed, and confident. His head was round and chunky unlike the typical wedge-shaped Siamese head. Plus, he was as dark and plump as a bon-bon with a little tub of a tummy. And could he talk! That is one of the things we loved that about Siamese: they are chatterboxes. We wanted cats that expressed themselves.

Three days after Donner came, Tristan arrived. He added a bit of action. Though he was named after a bold Wagnerian warrior, Tristan was clever enough to realize he was the "second cat." In just three days Donner had claimed the apartment as his territory. With a few casual, but well-aimed swipes of his paw, he let Tristan know it. Tristan must have accepted his role in cat body language because after a quick tussle or two, the two became forever buddies—but Donner was forever "top" cat. Tristan always positioned himself to the left and *slightly behind* Donner. It was his cagey way of walking the fine line between "second cat" status and his individual status as a personable, independent cat. Very subtly done, but Donner got the point. At any rate, Tristan got respect from him.

Caring for one cat is a lot of work but double the cats doubles the work, doubles the smelly kitty litter, doubles the battle when I had to ram deworming pills down their throats—double everything. This also included double love, affection, snuggling on the sofa, and sharing the day's events with Ward every evening. There wasn't a free moment to discuss Navy intelligence even if we had been allowed to.

By sharing both good times and bad with Donner and Tristan, we began to truly understand the pure love, joy, and sense of belonging to one another that is possible, and beautiful, between humans and cats. Although Ward and I weren't conscious of it, I believe in those wonderful three years, God was instilling in all of us—both humans and cats—the almost instinctive ability to understand when others are needy and to help them in any way we can. For example, when Donner or Tristan had a sudden need for extra attention, an especially vigorous scratch between the ears or a cuddle on my shoulder, I dropped everything to respond to their immediate needs. When Ward or I didn't feel well and took bed rest, both cats, especially Tristan, instinctively leaped to our side to provide the comfort of soft, warm cat fur around our necks.

Those three years passed quickly. Soon enough came the day when Ward received his next set of orders. As we had expected, they were in Washington, DC but these orders stunned us. We were to stop twice en route in Florida for Ward to attend specialty training in Naval Intelligence that would greatly enhance his career. It meant two months of travel and staying in bachelor officer quarters or motels.

But the cats! The cats! What about the cats! Our world turned topsy-turvy. I cried for three weeks as we planned to leave Germany and worried ourselves sick about what to do with the cats. Ward became grim and hardly spoke. Although neither of us thought to turn to God, He had already prepared us for this day.

Six months earlier, when Ward and I had taken a week's leave in Paris, Tristan and Donner stayed with our neighbors, the Randolfs. We returned to find them sprawled and purring on Fred Randolf's lap. They hadn't shed a tear. They hadn't stopped eating. They hadn't moped. Apparently, they hadn't missed us! Oh, back in our apartment, they wound themselves around our legs and butted their heads on our hands to welcome us home. But I was miffed. After all we did for them— to accept another home so easily! Traitors!

The truth of the matter is, the cats were happy at the Randolfs, and that is what really matters. Thus, we began to consider how the Randolfs literally were a Godsend. They were scheduled to stay in Germany for another eight years. They had fallen in love with the cats as deeply as we had. They begged us to give the cats to them.

I will never forget the day we kissed Donner and Tristan goodbye and turned toward the waiting taxi. In the plane over the Atlantic, I found myself whispering their names over and over. "Donner. Tristan. Donner. Tristan"…

Chapter 5

It had been five months since we kissed Donner and Tristan goodbye. Well established at work and home in Washington, DC, it was time to bring some Siamese into our home and hearts. In those days, the idea of Rescue pets wasn't as widespread as it is today. So, we did what we had to do and searched for a reliable breeder. Surely God had a hand in our search because we quickly found a cat breeder so wonderful, conscientious, loving, and careful about the people to whom she would entrust her precious cats that she should be the template for all breeders of all kinds of animals.

This paragon of the Siamese cat world, Eloise Forrestert, had rules of steel about to whom she would sell a kitten. No, no, not "sell" a kitten—how gauche! Rather, whom she deigned responsible enough to "adopt" one of her precious kittens. She first screened us over the phone. She listed her standards for prospective kitten owners. This included a written promise we would neuter the kittens, keep their shots up to date, and raise them as indoor cats. She made it very clear that for the kittens' optimum physical and emotional health, she would not separate them from their mother until they were nine weeks old. Only after we vowed to abide by these rules were we invited to visit.

That visit resulted in our taking into our home and hearts two kittens: a brother and sister, who in true Siamese fashion, began to chatter constantly from the minute they ambled out of the carrying case onto our oriental carpet.

Within an hour of tumbling into our living room, these tiny, charming creatures practically named themselves because their small but powerful personalities shone like lights in the darkness. The male's light was as strong as a lighthouse beam; the female's wasn't as dazzling, but cast a commanding, steady glow as if from a cluster of candles. Both kittens seemed right at home immediately. They weren't nervous, shy, or frightened as we had expected. We were delighted and attributed their self-assurance to the fact of their secure, loving kittenhood. Fear just wasn't in their vocabulary.

Ward noticed immediately the little guy had a firm, solid stance. We could imagine that if he had hips and hands, he'd be standing, tall and proud, with his hands on his hips like a winning prize fighter. "With that attitude, he reminds me of Taiho," Ward said, referring to one of Japan's top *sumo* wrestlers. And in that moment, in unison, we cried "Taiho!" And just like that, the little guy had a name.

We studied the female kitten, curled up with her chin nestled between her paws. She was so demure, so utterly feminine. She seemed the epitome of an oriental princess—instantly we knew she had to be named Michiko, the name of Japan's charming royal princess. Eventually, we would shorten it to Mikko, and even the less elegant Meeks and Squeako.

Another thing we noticed right away was, like Donner and Tristan, once again we had a "top cat" and a "second cat." As the kittens explored, Michiko was always a half step behind Taiho. She never took the initiative. She let him use the scratching post first. And the kitty litter first. She reminded me of an ancient, respectful Chinese wife, always trotting complacently behind her husband. When Taiho strode to the food dish, Michiko backed off, sat down, and waited patiently while Taiho attacked the food with the gusto of a starving barbarian. Occasionally he glanced up to ensure that Michiko was in her place.

She always was.

I made a silent vow to teach that young lady about equal rights and the ERA.

That delightful beginning of our lives with Taiho and Mikko continued, with ups and downs, for many wonderful years even as Ward's orders took us to Columbia, Maryland, The Pentagon, Hawaii, Japan, and back to Washington, DC. The cats endured all that travel as well as four months of quarantine in a special area of large, airy cages for pets in the hills of Hawaii.

As I look back on it, I realize this quarantine period exemplified in its own small way the challenge of Christianity, which is to recognize the suffering of others and take responsibility for relieving their misery. Taiho and Mikko weren't suffering the pangs of pain or hunger, but they were a lonely, unhappy little duo. I did my best to add a bit of love and comfort to their placid lives by visiting them every day. I admit I felt quite noble because it involved a long, rattling bus ride; a hike up a dusty hill in Hawaii's dry scrubland; and sitting cross-legged for hours in the cage with the cats.

I must also admit that saying the cats were unhappy is an understatement. They were bored and miserable. This was especially true for Taiho, whose gung-ho, lusty self-confidence disappeared without a trace. He literally turned his hunched back to me and huddled in the corner. No matter how I cajoled, pleaded, and offered tasty treats, he ignored me.

I cried a lot as I slouched in that cage. But wonder of wonders, sensitive Mikko seemed to recognize my suffering. She comforted me with every ounce of sympathy she had in her lithe, little body. She wriggled her way into my lap, butted me with her head, gazed longingly into my eyes, and even licked the tip of my nose with her soft, peach-fuzz tongue. She was, literally, a Godsend.

Ward visited the cats all sixteen weekends of their quarantine. His patience with Taiho was amazing. He talked softly to him as he slowly, slowly ran his fingers over Taiho's head. And finally, on Ward's fourth visit, it happened: Taiho's comeback!

Maybe God had seen enough of Taiho's intransigence. Maybe He had told Taiho to "get with it" because, without warning, Taiho made his move as Ward scratched between his ears. The cautious cat cocked his head, his eyes closed in seeming rapture, and he began to butt his head hard against Ward's hand. As we held our breath, he scrunched closer to Ward, finally oozing his way into Ward's lap as smoothly as flowing syrup. He tucked his paws under his chest, coiled his tail around his body—and burst into a rumbly purr. I suspect God smiled as broadly as I did.

Our Taiho was back! That evening we celebrated by splurging on dinner in one of Honolulu's finest restaurants—The Third Floor. So, while Taiho slept, curled with Mikko, high in Hawaii's dusty hills, we clinked glasses, sipped champagne, and giddily toasted our beloved Taiho, our champion Comeback Kid!..

Chapter 6

While our beloved cats were in quarantine in Hawaii, we were faced with a major decision: should we rescue a kitten? Who wouldn't? Well, there was a problem. The kitten in question was a seven-week-old pure white Himalayan, undoubtedly the sweetest, cutest kitten in Hawaii. She belonged to our next-door neighbor. The trouble was, at only seven weeks old, she had been given to a family that had a four-year-old boy whose idea of loving a kitten was to squeeze it in a death grip and screech joyfully into its ears. Within twenty-four hours the kitten was returned to her family of five brothers and sisters. Instead of greeting her like a prodigal sister and daughter, the whole family, including Mom, rejected her. When the kitten tried to enter their rough-and-tumble tug of war with an old sock, she was shouldered aside.

The first time I saw the kitten, she was a fluffy white ball huddled in a corner. In the opposite corner, her mother and littermates were nestled in a companionable, purring heap. I saw them through eyes blurred with tears. Ward, too, was struck through the heart by the loneliness of this tiny charmer. Although we ached to scoop her up and dash home with her, we kept our wits about us as we wondered how wise it was to introduce a new kitten to Taiho and Mikko when they returned from quarantine. Would they welcome her with open paws, or would she be rejected yet again? We consulted our Care of Cats book. We also consulted the veterinarian at the quarantine station. Finally, we shyly and hesitantly asked God for help and forgiveness for having forgotten Him for so long. We talked and argued all the pros and cons long into the night. We finally decided to adopt the kitten. We convinced ourselves things would work well if we introduced the cats gradually—first with a door between them, then with a screen, until they knew one another well enough to form a happy little trio.

And so, little Maile joined us two weeks before Taiho and Mikko were released from quarantine. After only one day of skittishness and caution, she settled between us on the sofa and pushed her purr to a roar. Smart kitten. She knew she had been rescued. Victory was hers! And with that, we knew her name must be Maile, the name of the vine ancient Hawaiians draped on the shoulders of winning athletes to symbolize victory. Maile hadn't won any races, but this plucky little kitten had overcome her fears and rejection. She was spirited! Victorious! She was Maile—and how we loved and treasured her!

You know that saying about mice and men and their best laid plans? They can often go astray—and that's what ours did. They went far astray from the moment that Taiho and Mikko were released from quarantine. We lovingly put the duo in our spare bedroom with their food, water, kitty litter, and toys. But despite all their familiar paraphernalia to comfort them, they were uneasy. Even with a door between them, Taiho and Mikko sensed there was an intruder in the house. In Siamese fashion, they yowled and howled and scratched and clawed the door until, in despair, we finally opened it a crack and they spotted the tiny invader. They were stunned. Their eyes narrowed, their backs arched, and they glared at me. Their looks spoke volumes: "Who is this? This puny kitten who acts like she owns the place"…

Chapter 7

Unfortunately, Maile—our Himalayan beauty— did act like she owned the place. Although she made a lively new feline companion with her gawky, kittenish leaps, when she bounded toward Taiho and Mikko it only seemed to annoy them. Taiho often exhibited his brutish growl (i.e. *"back off kid"*) toward her; plus, he would deliberately turn his back to her. Undeterred, Maile turned to Mikko, but our sweet, gentle Mikko shocked us by deliberately turning her regal head and gazing haughtily into the distance as if this spunky little intruder didn't exist.

It is painful to write about the next two months because no matter what we tried to ease the cats into accepting one another, nothing worked. Taiho, to our great distress, sank deeper and deeper into emotional and physical despair and desolation. Maile, for some unknown reason, possibly stress, suffered two bouts of debilitating diarrhea. And, yet in true Maile victorious fashion, she survived. The ever gentle, sensitive Mikko gradually accepted the fact Maile was here to stay. As a result, she made friendly advances to the kitten. In turn, Maile embraced these overtures with joy and gratitude. This was a Godsend because the day came when we had to euthanize Taiho, who was thirteen years old at the time.

It was the most difficult decision we had ever made, but I am convinced God guided us. For one, we followed the recommendation of the vet at the quarantine station, and we had contracted the services of a wonderful, compassionate veterinarian. Dr. Tanaka made home visits in her fully equipped vet clinic on wheels. She joined us in kissing Taiho goodbye, and weeping with us, before she skillfully, gently, and swiftly put Taiho to sleep. She offered to take Taiho to the quarantine station for cremation, but we chose to do it ourselves.

I will never forget that day. It was a lovely Hawaiian day of bright sunshine but as we turned off the main highway and headed uphill to the Quarantine Station, the windshield suddenly misted with the fine drops of a *mauka* ("mountain shower"). These quick Hawaiian showers that waft over the mountain tops are cool, welcome, and quite lovely. Then, suddenly ahead of us, brightening the mist with a glowing aura, a perfect rainbow arched across the sky. We drove directly under the high point of its arch as if we were taking Taiho to a place of mystical beauty. Tears blurred our vision as all our doubts dissolved. This welcoming sign in the heavens assured us that we had made the right decision. Our beloved and treasured Taiho was finally at peace.

In the following months and years, Maile and Mikko turned to one another and became forever buddies. Sweet Mikko sustained several illnesses and it was quite astounding for her to survive them. From a seventeen-year-old Wonder Cat, she went to an eighteen-year-old Miracle Cat; and at nineteen, her vet called her the Death-Defying Cat. One morning when she was nineteen-and-a-half, she collapsed in a soft heap on the kitchen floor. That afternoon, we held her for the last time and told her how much we loved her. Amazingly, she purred in our arms until our vet put her gently to sleep.

Maile lived on for two more years. She never became a lap cat, but she loved to burrow deep in the sofa cushions next to us—a little purring bundle of warmth against our thighs. When Maile was thirteen, we put her to sleep when an un-diagnosable illness wore her down to a shadow. We buried her next to Mikko in the woods behind our home. We wanted everything to be natural, so we marked both graves with crosses made of twigs. By now we were active members of the Episcopal Church; accordingly, we buried our little friends with solemn prayers for the dead.

At this point, twenty-five years had passed. The graves and crosses have returned to the soil. But the cats—all six of them—live on vividly in our memories and in our hearts…

Chapter 8

After all the cat funerals, life in our home was empty and lonely without a cat or two. Many evenings, Ward and I simply sat quietly on the sofa in our family room, holding one another and tearfully reminiscing in low, sad voices about the unique personalities of all our beautiful and loving kittens and cats. For days and weeks on end, we pondered the question of whether to adopt two more Siamese kittens from a nearby rescue shelter. We made a pros and cons list, but no matter how we tried to boost the pro side, the practicalities and realities of our life always added weight to the con side. After all, Ward was about to retire after thirty-two years in Naval Intelligence. We were bursting with plans to travel the world. Would it be fair to leave cats in boarding kennels for long stretches? And the big question: what would happen eight or ten years down the road when we planned to move to a retirement community? Do they allow cats? Would our age and health allow us to ferry the cats to the vet or handle simple, everyday matters such as shopping for cat food and twenty-five-pound boxes of kitty litter?

Sadly, we decided not to adopt any more cats. I remember the night we made this decision. It was deathly still that night in our home. Ward couldn't sit still. He was up and down, pacing, opening and closing the refrigerator door just to stare blankly inside. I was on a cleaning streak. Put simply, I scrubbed. I scrubbed everything in sight—the sink, the microwave, the cabinet doors. And as I scrubbed, I cried, quietly, a river of tears.

Time passed as it always does, and when Ward finally retired, he became an enthusiastic travel planner, organizer, and researcher. Our hopes and dreams to see the world came true. Thanks to the Navy having sent us to duty stations hither and yon, we had already visited more than a dozen countries. During the next twenty-seven years we flew, sailed, cruised, trained, drove, and trotted across the globe. Ward racked up 106 countries. I was a sluggard with only ninety-six.

In 2010, we moved into a sunny, thirteenth floor apartment of a faith-based retirement community— which *did* allow small pets! It was a propitious move because Ward had developed Chronic Obstructive

Pulmonary Disease [COPD] that required increasing medical care. Eleven years later, Ward's COPD developed into pneumonia that took a terrible toll on his body.

At age eighty-three, he died quietly on January 1, 2021. I was blessed to be with him, and doubly blessed our priest was there to give Ward Last Rites. Those Rites, in which the dying Christian's soul is received into the arms of God with assurance of eternal life, saved me from crumbling into complete despair. Nevertheless, from a spirited extrovert, I sank into lethargic hopelessness. Alone, with no children and no family nearby, with no one to travel with or confide in, I had no reason to get up in the morning. I didn't have a goal. I slept a lot. I hung around in my pajamas. The only positive thing I did was to print the Last Rites and post them on my kitchen cabinet where I read them many times a day, trying to console myself.

Meanwhile, in an apartment at the other end of the hallway, another drama was unfolding as Marjorie, my kind and caring friend and neighbor, suddenly became ill. Marjorie was an ardent animal lover—especially cats. She supported and volunteered at several animal shelters, and at this time, she owned a rescue cat named

Cora. Marjorie's illness and trips to various hospitals upended life in her apartment. Family, nurses, food deliverers, and friends came and went. A hospital bed was set up in the living room. Through all this turmoil, Cora retreated to the refuge of a dark closet in the spare bedroom. Marjorie's friends, including me, stopped by to refresh Cora's food, water, and kitty litter.

As days and weeks went by, and as people continued to come and go, little Cora built a protective shell around herself. At mealtimes she walked cautiously close to the wall to her food bowl with her head down as if trying to disappear. As soon as she finished, she slunk back to her closet to hunch in sleep or just stare into the dimness. Just once she allowed me to briefly stroke her head. Cora was a small, handsome Tabby cat whose fur was a soft blend of gray with black, brown, and russet with touches of silver-pearl. However, without her usual daily care, this beautiful fur was becoming scruffy and matted.

As I watched Cora retreat both physically and emotionally, I puzzled over the next step. Before Marjorie had adopted Cora from the shelter, she had wisely thought ahead to what would become of Cora if she, Marjorie, were to die first. Knowing I am also an ardent cat person, Marjorie asked me to take Cora if it became necessary. I immediately agreed. Of course, I'd care for a sweet cat who had endured many upheavals in her life. Marjorie was her third owner. Cora's background was unknown. At this point, so was her future. Would Marjorie recover? Or was she nearing the end of her long, inspirational life?

Two or three weeks later Marjorie made her painful decision and told her daughter, Donna, that it was time to give Cora up. From my own experience of losing or giving up a beloved cat, I understood the depth of Marjorie's heartbreak as she kissed Cora goodbye. She then handed her to Donna, who loved Cora as dearly as her mother did. Donna did not immediately hand Cora to me. She wanted to hold her until the last minute. "I'll carry her to your apartment," she said.

We walked down the hallway together with a puzzled, squirming little cat in Donna's arms. As I looked at Cora, I sped a quick prayer to heaven. "Dear God, two lives are beginning anew. Guide us, please. I suspect we may we calling on you a lot." And, with that, my life changed…

Chapter 9

When we entered my apartment, Cora seemed to understand this was another new home—her fifth including her shelter days. She stopped squirming and pulled herself tighter to Donna. She squeezed her eyes shut and tucked her head into Donna's jacket. Donna was crying while I stood stock-still, although every nerve in my body was quivering. I seemed to be able to sense Cora's fears. I could almost hear her pitiful, inner cries. *What's happening? Where's Marjorie? Is this a new place?*

The instant Donna lowered Cora to the floor in my living room, the terrified cat scrambled to hunker under an end table. She sank as far from me as possible. She pressed so tightly against the wall that I was surprised she didn't make a dent in it. Overwhelmed by emotion, with a final air kiss for Cora and a hug for me, Donna fled—leaving Cora and me to get acquainted.

And so, there we were: the two of us, eyeing one another. Cora was still hunched and ominously silent under the end table. My heart went out to her, and in a leap of love, I made a wrong move. Holding firm to the table leg, I painstakingly lowered myself to my knees. By bending over I was able to stretch my arm out toward Cora under the table. There! I felt a bit of fur. But the next thing I felt were Cora's teeth in my thumb. For a ninety-year-old woman, I moved with Olympic speed to jump to my feet and inspect my wound. I was stunned. In all our years of caring for cats, I'd only been bitten—a tiny bite—once by Max the Balcony Cat. This was a shock. My mind raced. What to do? Try to stanch the blood or encourage the flow to purge any germs. I decided to pinch the base of my thumb to encourage the flow. Thankfully, I remembered that Cora's rabies vaccination was up to date.

Emotionally exhausted, I sank onto the sofa and sat, unmoving, eyes blurred by tears, contemplating what to do about that trembling heap of scruffy fur. And Cora certainly was scruffy. All those weeks in the closet without petting or grooming had destroyed the lustrous thick beauty of a healthy tabby cat's coat. Without brushing, her fur had become shabby and colorless and matted like hard gray felt. In some places the matting was as solid and large as a walnut. The clump of fur under her chin had tangled into a cluster of knots, which made her face look very surly. However, I would later happily discover, when not terrified, Cora had a sweet, pleasant face. Her head was shaped in a wide triangle with her yellow-green eyes slightly slanted at the broadest part, which, when she was at ease gave her a softness that made her adorable— almost kittenish. At the tip of the triangle was a dewy patch of white fur around her nose, mouth, and chin. This certainly lent her a coquettish charm.

During the previous weeks when I had fed Cora during Marjorie's terminal illness, I had been distressed by the lonely, disheveled little cat—so much so my heart strings were already tightly tugged by the needy little tyke. Now that she was here, frightened and shivering and in my care, I was overpowered by love— a love expressed in the old hymn, as "how deep, how broad, how high." I knew her bite was her only defense in a fearful situation. I could imagine how terrified that sweet, helpless cat was.

At that moment my soul and the sunlit room were flooded by a peaceful presence. A warmth—a softness—enfolded us and I straightened up as I sensed the gentleness and quiet presence of God in the room with Cora and me. I was certain He was gifting us to one another. That precious, if messy, little cat was God's special gift to me! The moment was so profound my breath shuddered as I suddenly understood God was actively taking a hand to fulfill both of our needs: my need for a purpose, a reason to pursue a meaningful life; Cora needed attention— not just a good haircut, medications, and grooming, but hugs, soft and gentle words, and loving scratches under her chin.

As the blood stopped welling out and the small sharp pain of her bite diminished, the transcendental moment lingered, then slowly faded. Once again, I breathed normally; however, I sat as still as a statue not wanting to release this sense of wonder. Since then, I have thought of it often. I am constantly amazed—and grateful—that in the vastness of His universe God took special care to understand our individual needs and unite the team of Cora and me. I really shouldn't be amazed. The answer is simple. We are His creatures, and He loves us.

That evening I had a crazy thought. It was the height of COVID-19 pandemic. We, the denizens of the Goodwin House Bailey's Crossroads, a faith-based retirement community, were staying close to our own apartments. We socialized informally with three or four of us getting together in the elevator lobby to share a glass of wine now and then. These groups became known as "pods." Within your own pod you felt comfortable enough to remove your mask to sip your wine. Marjorie had been in my pod. At any rate, my crazy thought was this: "Hey, Cora, we're in a three-person pod—you, me, and God!" The thought of it gave me shivers –and a chuckle. But when I told Cora, she didn't even twitch an ear. She just kept chowing down on Meow Mix.

"Cora, you're in a pod with *God*!" I repeated, loudly, next to her deaf ear. No response. Just the crunch of Meow Mix. I rolled my eyes. But I wasn't worried about any heavenly punishment for this stubborn little sinner. God's feelings weren't hurt. He understood that most cats believed they were His equal—and He lovingly allowed them a bit of leeway, which Cora graciously accepted as her due.

Even though Cora's rabies shots were up to date, and a nurse in our clinic gave me an antibiotic, I kept an eye on the small puncture wound on my thumb. It healed quickly. Nevertheless, I decided to wear some "armor" whenever I attempted to touch Cora. Lacking some good old medieval chain metal, for two weeks I armored myself with heavy leather gloves and my winter jacket with zip-in lining. As Cora adjusted to my light touch on her head, I felt confident enough to remove the jacket lining and downgrade my glove defense to white cotton gloves. A couple of weeks later, as Cora gradually realized that I wouldn't harm her, I discarded the jacket and gloves, but continued to wear tops with long sleeves. I couldn't quite shake the memory of Cora's fierce hiss and tiny, sharp fangs. The downgrading of the armor was one of the subtle ways I kept track of Cora's progress toward a warm, loving alliance with me.

Wearing cat armor, however, was a simple matter compared to dealing with one of Cora's medications called gabapentin. I both loved and hated it. I loved it because it calmed Cora before a visit to the vet; I hated it because—well, it's a long story. Let me explain . . .

Among other things, gabapentin relieves anxiety. I had never heard of it until Cora's veterinarian prescribed it for her whenever Cora had to travel in the deluxe carrier Marjorie had bought for her. You see, the vet—to put it mildly—described Cora as "feisty." Thus, the gabapentin wasn't just for Cora's anxiety when she saw the carrier; it was to knock her out cold.

I'm sure I hated Cora's gabapentin days as much, or even more, than she did. The medication required specific timing; for example, Cora couldn't have any food for fifteen hours before her medical or grooming appointments, except for one tablespoon of "tuna juice" in which the gabapentin was dissolved three hours before the appointment. To stick to this schedule, I made a time chart of this and posted it in the kitchen. The schedule called for removing Cora's dry food bowl during the night, which deprived her of her nightly nibbles. This meant that in the morning, I faced a very hungry and confused cat. From the looks she tossed my way, I knew she blamed me for her empty tummy.

With one frightening exception I'll explain later, Cora quickly lapped her allotted tablespoon of tuna juice in which the gabapentin was dissolved. She then sniffed around for more food, winding herself between my feet, her puzzled face and whole body pitifully pleading for something to eat. I could barely stand it. The sweet little girl was starving! I recalled the pathetic scene in the orphanage when starving little Oliver Twist bravely raises his porridge bowl and pleads, "Please sir, I want some more."

The first time I gave gabapentin to Cora, I had no idea what to expect, so I kept a close watch on her as she wandered aimlessly around the apartment. Maybe it wasn't aimless. Maybe she was sniffing out any food that may have been dropped, or even searching for a stray mouse, which wasn't too likely in my thirteenth-floor apartment. But eventually, after a half hour or so, Cora's legs began to wobble and slip on the kitchen tiles. I watched with tears welling in my eyes. I couldn't bear it. She looked so pitiful and puzzled. What was happening to her? She fought on, but shortly those little legs gave up; she slumped sideways and slid to the floor. With as much tenderness as I could summon, I picked up her surprisingly heavy dead weight and cradled her in her carrier. Ideally, as pitiful as it appeared, this was how the gabapentin was supposed to work every time. And it did except for the one frightening exception that I mentioned.

It happened the day Cora had a routine check-up appointment with the vet. She had already gone twelve hours without food. It was time for the gabapentin in tuna juice. Although she must have been starving, for some crazy reason, this kooky little cat refused the gabapentin—even in a double dose of tuna juice. I tried two other tempting foods, including wild Alaskan salmon, for which I opened a $3.00 can.

When I pleaded with her and held each offering one inch from her mouth, she finally deigned to sample a smidgen of each of the tempting tidbits. But after one quick swipe of her pink tongue over each one, she turned her back, and with the swaying of her jaunty little butt, she flounced away. No, I'm wrong. Cora didn't flounce. Cora was not a flouncy cat like our egotistical Petrouchka. Cora merely walked away—*stubbornly.*

I rescheduled her appointment. Then, emotionally exhausted and smelling faintly of fish, I made some coffee and settled down to finish the newspaper while Cora groomed herself in her sunny corner window. About a half hour later, there was Cora in the middle of the kitchen staggering in circles on wobbly legs. Over and over, she lost her balance and fell on her side. It was heartbreaking to watch her try to get up, as her legs fanned out from under her. I was frozen in horror with no idea of what to do. For a moment I relaxed as Cora managed to crawl twelve to fifteen inches to her food bowl and nibble a few dry Meow Mix crunchies, even as her hind legs kept slipping out from under her. Suddenly she collapsed completely; all four of her legs splayed out so her body lay flat on the floor like a furry letter X. It was terrifying.

I cried out Cora's name over and over as my mind raced—should I rush her to the animal emergency hospital? She was dying. I was sure of it. I crouched over her, crying to God to help us.

I couldn't just leave her on the hard floor, so I scooped her up and carried her to the sofa. If she were dying, at least she would be on soft cushions. As I carried her limp, dead weight, my mind cleared a bit. I was struck by the possibility that Cora's reaction may have been due to the small amount of gabapentin she had ingested when she licked the food. And with that thought, my mood lightened. It lightened some more when I thought of how, despite her grogginess, Cora had dragged herself to the food bowl and nibbled a bit. I doubted dying cats lusted for food. It had to be that smidgen of gabapentin.

The upshot was that I stayed on the sofa with her for a couple of hours until she awakened, yawned, stretched, and then sort of half tumbled down her special cat steps. She then ventured further on stronger, but still-wobbly legs to her beloved water bowl. Later, as I tempted her with treats, she climbed the steps to the sofa by herself, gobbled the treats, and tucked her nose into my side and slept. Oh my!

I wept. When I had thought she was dying, I was desperate. I loved her so very much; to see her with her eyes glazed over, with no strength in her body, was unbearable. My heart can take just so much fright, and the sight of that kooky little cat as a flattened, furry X on the floor was pushing it to its limits. Thank goodness, I never again saw her as a flat, furry X on the floor…

Chapter 10

For the next month Cora and I carefully checked out one another. I gazed at her with the same love and affection that had swept over me at the first sight of her huddled under my table. She, on the other hand, sized me up through squinting, doubting eyes. Not that I saw those eyes very often, for Cora had a habit of keeping her head lowered most of the time. Marjorie had told me about it, and we had wondered why.

Had something in her kittenhood made her fearful of facing the world? Or was it a physical problem with her neck? No, that couldn't be. She looked up when I filled her food bowl and held it close to her nose to tell her it was dinner time. There was no point in calling her or ringing the dinner bell because of her deafness. So, I treasured every momentary glimpse of her face. I ached with pity wondering what abuse Cora may have endured long ago to make her seem so fearful.

Because Ward and I had raised our Siamese cats from kittenhood in a secure, loving home, they grew into normal, fun-loving cats. They wrestled with one another, they jumped in and out of paper bags, they tried to capture the Cuckoo in our German clock, they nestled in our laps, around our necks, and batted ornaments from the Christmas tree. Cora, on the other hand, was a mystery. Where had she come from? What kind of treatment had she experienced? Her medical record reported damaged paws in her younger days from ingrown nails. What else may she have suffered from uncaring owners?

The very thought broke my heart. I recognized much of my love for Cora was entwined with pity. That realization strengthened my belief that God had a definite purpose in sending her to me so her golden years would be sweet ones. I wasn't sure of her age. Her medical records had conflicting dates of her birth. I figured that she was around thirteen—a very tiny thirteen.

I treasured every inch of that tiny, needy thirteen-year-old body. And so, within five minutes of her entering my life, I was transformed from an idle, hapless human being into, if not exactly a whirlwind of activity, at least a brisk breeze with a purpose in life, which was to square away this shaggy little cat within a few days. I would have to have her matted hair shaved, nails clipped, checked by her vet, vaccinated for rabies, and medicated with amoxicillin. But most of all, I tried to give Cora what she most needed: petting, love, comfort, and a sense of security. She had lost all of that when she lost Marjorie. I knew God's assignment to me was to love her with every fiber of my being. If only all God's requests were as effortless as this.

While I was transformed from idleness to a purposeful life, Cora was physically transformed. After being professionally shaved, her body was sleek and dull gray—sort of like the body of a mouse. The poor little thing looked awkward, thin, and cold, a skinny little bit of a cat with pointy knees, elbows, and shoulders. They looked particularly frail in contrast to the full mane or ruff that framed her face because of her Lion's Cut grooming. I didn't dare laugh at her, and I kept her away from mirrors. No point in embarrassing her.

When she curled tightly to sleep, she looked shivery cold. I searched my apartment for a covering that was warm but lightweight. And wouldn't you know? It turned out to be my best shawl: a gorgeous pink one that was 50% pashmina silk and 50%

cashmere. I tucked it around Cora. She snuggled in. With her tiny, triangular face peeking from the pink folds, she looked too adorable for words. "Okay sweetie, it's yours," I murmured in her ear. "You are now the only cat in northern Virginia with her very own pink pashmina shawl."

Cora shrugged a bit, settling herself more snugly into the shawl. It was a nonchalant shrug that said, "Thanks. It's comfy. But, please, no more talking. I need sleep."

Cora and her pink pashmina shawl became a pair. I tucked her into it every night, and she wriggled in to her comfort level. She must have felt protected by its light, but warm weight. She even used it when her fur grew back out to a lustrous coat of black and brown with tints of silver-gray. Her coat also had lustrous streaks of reddish bronze when the sun highlighted it, which was often because my living room seemed to have been made for sun-worshipping cats like Cora…

Chapter 11

My apartment consists of a living-dining room, two bedrooms, kitchen, den and two bathrooms. It is at the end of a 60-foot-long hallway on the thirteenth floor of our retirement home. The living room is oddly shaped. It comes to a point where two floor to ceiling windows meet, which offers a wide view that includes a busy neighborhood and stretches all the way to the airport. Cars, planes, and people offer variety, and the sun warms that inviting corner most of the day. It must have been designed by a cat person. It became Cora's haven. Early on, she sat, hunched, looking out. But as she acclimated to our life together and trusted that I wouldn't grab her with evil intent when she wasn't on guard, she began to sprawl in the sun in the corner.

What a pleasure to see her lightly sun-burnished, lush, tabby cat coat on her relaxed, sleeping body. Sometimes she raised her chin and rested it on the window frame as if in homage to the sun, but mostly she lowered her head to her chest and covered her eyes with a curled paw. This is an especially adorable position for all cats. I wonder if they do it on purpose. Cora's relaxed, open positions often brought tears to my eyes because they showed she trusted me completely. What a change from the fearful, miserable, matted cat whom God had sent into my apartment and my heart months earlier.

At first, I didn't dare touch her legs or paws. The first time I tried, she instantly hissed, glared, sharp-eyed at me and jerked her limbs back under her body. When I tried again a month later, she merely gave me a reproving look—a small but meaningful step in our developing relationship.

More and more often Cora slept in a flung-out position in a wide half-circle with her legs stretched at full length with her tummy exposed. When she slept like that in the middle of the living room instead of under a table or out-of-the-way corner, it was yet another sign of her assurance of her safety in her new home. She was so endearing I had to fight an overwhelming desire to scoop her up and hug her against my cheek.

Once, I lowered myself to the floor with some ninety-one-year-old-lady grunts and put my face near Cora's ear and whispered, "Hi little sweetheart. I love you so very much. Sleep well. You're safe." I must admit sometimes I was even gushier and called Cora "my sweet Baboo." The first time I did that, Cora opened her eyes in surprise, and I could practically hear her thoughts:

> *Oh boy, here she is again, interrupting my divine sleep in the sun, and calling me that silly name, "Sweet Baboo." I was in the middle of a dream about that new canned food she bought yesterday: "Alaska Salmon ala Florentine with fresh garden vegetables in a delicate sauce." Gourmet stuff! She clapped her hands with delight and called me "good, good girl" when I ate all of it and meowed for more. She seems to think I did something special.*

> *She's a little weird sometimes, like last night when she praised me to the skies when all I had was a solid poop after a couple of days of not-so-solid. But besides being a little weird, she's soft-hearted. She seems to think I like being sung to. Well, I do. I love it. Seems like all she knows is "Amazing Grace." It always puts me to sleep though. A little variety would be nice,*

especially since she only knows the first verse.

Anyway, back to her disturbing my sleep. Well, to be truthful, she didn't disturb it on purpose. I just felt the vibes on the wooden floor when she came up close. In fact, she didn't touch a hair on my body. She just sat and watched me for a long time, and she talked out loud about me, as if she were writing something in her head about me. It made me feel embarrassed, but I didn't let on. I saw her through squinched eyes. She had such a loving look on her face, and she said thank you to someone she called God for me. She called me a "gift." Me? A gift? Wow! Whad'Ya know? Once she clasped her hands to her chest and sighed that she did not know how she could contain all the love and awe and wonder that seemed to want to burst out of her. I was a little worried about that one, but she calmed down, so I didn't think I had to wake up and comfort her. Besides, she unclasped her hands and began writing in a notebook. So, I un-squinched my eyes and went back to sleep. I trusted her not to touch my exposed tummy. She's been very good about that ever since I bit her to let her know that I have my dignity. And yes, I bit her harder than I wanted to, and I'm sorry about that. I butt her hand a lot with my head to let her know that I'm sorry and that I love her. Now, back to sleep in the lovely sun in my corner window.

As Cora slept and dreamed, I watched her tummy and chest breathe easily in and out. I thought about what she had gone through in her younger years. The veterinarian's notes from those days were scant. I knew only she had never really had a "forever home," and that sometime in her past her paws had been damaged due to ingrown toenails. I couldn't bear the thought of her ever being in pain. As I often did when I watched her sleep, I sent a thank you to God for this little furry bundle who was beginning to toddle to greet me when I returned to the apartment. I chuckled to myself imagining Cora's thoughts upon my return. Did she come to me out of love, affection, trust? Or was it, "Oh good, here is my cat food can opener person" or "Here's the crazy lady who is a great chin stroker, but who is always singing 'Amazing Grace' but only verse 0ne. I wish she'd learn more"? It is true, my friends. Although I never did learn more verses, I believe those sunny, quiet moments enriched my life with more than my share of amazing grace…

Chapter12

When Cora came to live with me, she was accompanied by her litter box and two bags of kitty litter. I had forgotten about the horrible sight of kitty litter. I had many smelly memories of it that made my stomach clutch in horror. Instantly, I recalled our long-ago kitty litter adventures in Germany. In those days, litter wasn't much better than sand. In Germany, I swore it came straight from the windblown, unkempt banks of the Weser River. When I poured it into the litter box, it billowed in the air in clouds of gritty, pore-clogging dust that settled in a fine beige film on the furniture. When the cats' urine turned the sand to mud, the apartment smelled of ammonia, but at least I didn't have to tiptoe barefoot in it as Tristan and Donner did.

How they hated it! They quickly learned the only time it was relatively clean and dry was when it was freshly poured. At the first sizzle of pouring litter that alerted them to a fresh load, they raced to the box to sit beside it until it was ready for use. They were like a comedy team. Their eyes were closed to slits against the dust. They sneezed, small, but messy sneezes. They shook their heads in annoyance and rubbed their faces with curled paws. They suffered briefly for the joy of crouching occasionally in clean litter. They were so ecstatic they practically purred as they peed.

When the litter was not perfectly clean, Tristan showed me how cats can be imaginative and inventive. With a determined look on his face, he backed up to the corner of the litter box and slowly, breathtakingly, one leg at a time, lifted all four legs to perch—*backward* on the corner edge of the box. To me it was a wondrous, precarious balancing act. I was amazed by the clever little cat whose body was tense with concentration to balance his butt over the litter as he did his business before jumping down and walking away. Naturally I cheered and was rewarded with a smug, nose-in-the-air smile.

And now, forty-five years later, here was Cora and her memory-stirring kitty litter. But wait! Boy, had kitty litter changed in those years. One word on the bag made my spirits soar: "Clumping." I was thrilled to learn that clumping litter was "fast absorbing" so it made "tight, hard clumps for easy scooping, with low dust and tracking." Incredible! My pulse quickened. And there was even more. This miracle product had "odor control and a light, fresh scent that was paw-activated!" Paw-activated! Wow! To top off this sensational event, like the cherry on top of the cake, Cora remembered where I put the litter box and used it from her first day with me. Could life get any better?

With happy thoughts, I reconfigured Ward's bathroom into Cora's Retreat with her litter box at one end and her beloved large red and white water bowl at the other end. I say "beloved" because Cora seemed to have a strong affection for that bowl. Maybe she knew that it had served two of Marjorie's rescue cats and held fond memories. Or maybe her fondness for it was that it was big. It held two and a half cups of water; Cora was a water-holic. If she wasn't sleeping or eating, she was guzzling water as if she expected a drought any minute.

Cora didn't really guzzle. She was far too ladylike for that—and too fastidious to lean over and drink from the middle of the bowl, risking getting her chest wet. She chose to lap at the rim of the bowl with her tiny, quick-darting pale pink tongue. Her refined style resulted in rivulets of water sliding down the sides of the bowl onto the tile floor, and the kooky cat barely noticed her paws were wet. She quickly and casually shook them and walked away.

Months later, as she became confused, she walked through her water bowl; in turn, that made her paws ripe for picking up clingy bits of stray kitty litter, which immediately hardened between her toes and pricked her soft pink pads. When I first got her, before she was groomed, I could hear Cora's paws clicking on the hardwood floor—a combination of long nails and hardened kitty litter. I tried to imagine what she was going through. I knew the misery of having just a grain of sand in my shoe. While waiting three days for Cora's grooming appointment at the pet salon, I tried my best to help her; when she was sound asleep—and she was a champion deep sleeper—I carefully explored the clumps of litter that clung like lichen in rough, leather-like platelets to her fur and wedged between her toes. I tried to detach bits off the edge of this leathery patch by pinching and rolling tiny bits between my fingertips until a miniscule ball broke away, carrying with it a microscopic fluff of fur. During the five tense minutes it took to clean one teensy scrap of litter, my heart melted, and tears flooded my vision. This was a job for Cora's groomer who told me that I was not alone;

thousands of cat owners wanted to know how to remove kitty litter from between their cat's toes.

After that emotionally exhausting afternoon of trying to de-litter Cora's toes, Cora rewarded my efforts by purring for thirty minutes as she tucked into my lap while I sang hymns. Cuddling and hymn singing were becoming a nightly routine for God's needy duo. But something still had to be done about the clumping kitty litter…

Chapter 13

Once again, I was at the pet salon to pick up Cora after her complete grooming. "I suggest you try a non-clumping kitty litter," Cora's groomer advised me. "Non-clumping is messier to clean, but it may not clump as easily between Cora's toes." Wonderful advice. However, because of her matted undercoat, she had required another Lion Cut, the same cut she had had several months earlier when she came to live with me. The cut, which frees the cat from itchy matting and keeps them cool in hot weather, involves trimming all a cat's fur except a lion-like ruff around the neck and five pompoms on the feet and tail.

The first time the groomer showed me Cora with her Lion Cut, I was stunned. I held in my laughter though. It would have embarrassed the poor, shorn little cat. Although the Lion Cut is the most popular hair cut for cats, it didn't do a thing for Cora's appearance. Cats are told they look lionesque with this cut. It assuages the indignity of being shorn of their luxurious fur except for their spiky ruff and five silly pompoms. I couldn't honestly tell Cora that she looked lionesque. She looked more Disney-mousesque, for under her deep coat of matted fur she was skinny with pointy shoulders and hip bones that looked so fragile, it seemed they might snap. Her close cut revealed that she was mostly a gray tabby. As I held in my giggles, my heart ached for such a tiny, puny little creature.

My heart was also heavy. I felt foolish because I was responsible for Cora needing this second Lion Cut. I had not been brushing her properly. As her lustrous gray-black-reddish tabby hair grew back after her first Lion Cut, I thought I was doing the best for her by brushing her with both sides of her special brush that had both metal teeth and semi-soft bristles. I didn't know I should have been combing her undercoat until one day, as I stroked her, I felt lumps matting under the top layer of thick, long hair!

I tried to comb it out, gently backstroking it. Cora seemed to enjoy some of the gentle pull of the brush until her muscles tensed and her squint-eyed look said, "Hey, this is more hair pulling than I bargained for." And so, it was off to the pet salon where, in addition to the Lion Cut, I also got the kitty litter advice to use non-clumping litter.

It turns out the groomer was right. The non-clumping litter did not harden between Cora's toes, but it was messier, heavier, and smellier. Cleaning the litter box was now a bigger chore, as I could no longer take a small bag of clumps to the trash room at the end of the hall and pitch them down the trash chute. Now I had to muster all my strength to tip the messy litter from the litter box to a super big trash bag. It was too heavy for me to lug down the long corridor, so I wheeled it down on the seat of my rolling office chair. I performed this herculean task in my pajamas at midnight to avoid meeting neighbors.

After that, whenever I saw Cora using the litter box—easily shaking the non-clumping litter from her paws—I reminded her I had assumed extra work just to keep her clean and comfortable. I could have been talking to the moon for all the response I got. Alas, she was better for it, so I blew her a kiss anyway …

Chapter 14

Anyone who knows cats knows they can be inscrutably kooky. At times Cora was kooky to the hilt. For example, she was too small, old, and arthritic to jump up onto my large black leather sofa. But, oh, she tried. As she eyed the smooth black leather cliff facing her and assumed a pounce position, I could almost feel waves of determination rising from her quivering body. Then came the leap—the old college try. Each time she sprang, she fell backward. Her arthritic legs gave out and her toenails couldn't snag the smooth leather to give her a hold. Of course, she pretended she wasn't embarrassed—that it didn't make any difference. As in the old Nat King Cole song, she simply "picked herself up, dusted herself off, and started all over again."

I didn't dare let her see me laughing.

After a couple of days of watching her desperate attempts and tumbles, I bought a pet stair with three steps. These pet stairs were supposedly a lifeline for arthritic pets. I hoped it would spare her the embarrassment of lacking well-known cat-like grace.

I admit I was excited about the three-step stair, so I was stunned when Cora took one suspicious look at it and backed off. She wouldn't even sniff it to give it a chance. As she sat glowering at it from three feet away, I could read her thoughts: *Now what? Changes. Always changes.*

Well, I was not about to be defeated by a twelve-pound cat.

I had my own tactics involving Cora's insane weakness for a special cat treat that was crunchy on the outside and soft in the center. I usually gave her four or five of these while I ate my own dinner. Knowing this chink in her armor, I put a handful of these treats into a small bowl and placed it on the bottom step.

Crunchy treats! Cora could not resist. Her nose twitched and her body quivered as she slunk up to the treats. But I was quicker and moved the bowl to the second stair. Cora still came on. But when I moved the bowl to the top step, that was too much for her. She stopped. She tilted her head and studied the bowl.

"Oh, come on, Cora," I pleaded. "Come up the steps, or the treats will go away." With that, I moved the bowl onto the sofa, far back to where Cora couldn't see it.

Zoom! Like a lighting streak Cora was up the stairs and attacking the treats while I cheered. Finally, she had accepted the stairs!

Well, my clarion cry of triumph was premature. For the rest of Cora's life, she had a love/hate relationship with those steps. When it suited her, she used them to go up and down, but most of the time, she eyed them with disdain, and gave them a wide berth. I wondered if her dismissal of them was like my disdain for a cane. Were both of us fighting signs of aging?

Another of Cora's kooky cat antics involved her feline ancestry. Cora would not drink from her water bowl unless it was far from her food dish. In Marjorie's apartment, Cora's food had been in the kitchen. Her water was two rooms away in the bathroom. It was strange to watch her trudge back and forth two or three times during a meal. Not knowing why she preferred this arrangement I decided when Cora came to live with me, all three of her bowls—wet food, dry food, and water bowl—would be under the kitchen table where she could feel secure and out-of-the-way. But Cora had other plans. She attacked her food bowls with gusto but ignored her water.

After twenty-four hours of Cora not drinking, I, much worried, took to the Internet to try to find an answer. And there it was! Cora's feline ancestors in the wild instinctively kept their food and water far apart to "prevent contamination from bacteria and other sources." Cora had inherited this deep instinct. I immediately moved her water bowl to my late husband's bathroom. Her kitty litter box was in one corner, but apparently the water was far enough away from it to be acceptable, for as soon as I moved the bowl, Cora drank…and drank…and drank. From then on, she trudged back and forth during her meals. To see her little body plod from food to drink and back again, I felt myself pulled, truly pulled, by an enigmatic tenderness toward this little creature who, herself, was pulled by primal instincts.

I'll never know if it was primal instinct or deep-down hunger at the core of one of Cora's kookiest moments. She had been with me for over a month, enough time for us to establish a schedule and a basic understanding of one another. I had fed Cora and was preparing my own dinner; I liked to eat sitting on the floor at the coffee table while I watched the TV news. I eased my creaky bones onto a pillow at the low table with my back against the sofa. Then I turned to place Cora's small plate with five crunchy treats on the seat of the sofa. My own meal was also a treat—sautéed shrimp, noodles, and snow peas that I ordered "to go" from our community café.

My head was bowed, and I was in the middle of saying grace when I felt a weight on one shoulder. Then, I felt a weight on the other shoulder. Unbelievable! They were Cora's paws, and soon they were trying to scramble over my head to get to my shrimp. I half turned and tried to nudge her back onto the sofa, but all twelve pounds of her little body fought me. She threw most of her weight over my left shoulder; her hind paws pushed to gain traction on my shoulder blades as she fought and twisted and wrestled with me. I was stunned by the strength and determination in that tiny body as she fought me for my shrimp.

Fighting me! Imagine! This quiet little old cat had gumption. I loved it. Even as I shouted, "No, Cora, no!" and pushed back at her, trying to grab her fierce little body, I was laughing so hard I barely had the strength to defend my shrimp. *Defend my shrimp! From little Cora of all things!* That idea made me laugh harder.

I finally untangled myself. With groaning effort, I rose, snatched up my plate and, still laughing, sat down to recover.

Cora, also exhausted, hunched on the sofa, and stared at my shrimp on a higher table out of her range.

"You little villain," I chuckled at her. "You kooky little cat. You have no manners, but I love your guts."

Cora just stared at the shrimp.

Soon after, I cut a shrimp into small pieces and piled them on Cora's personal plate. She earned those pieces of shrimp and devoured them without so much as a thankful glance. That kooky little girl never again showed such spunk. I missed it. I had enjoyed that spark of life. It's one of my strongest memories of that tiny precious gift from God...

Chapter 15

In all our years of living with cats, my husband and I never sang to them, so I don't know if they liked music. Cora, on the other hand, enjoyed music and had a favorite hymn, "Amazing Grace." How did I know? Funny you should ask . . .

Well, I'm not a singer but I love music, especially my favorite hymns that I sing as I do household chores. It's fun and pleasing but in practical terms, it helps me to cope with a medical problem called Musical Ear Syndrome [MES]. It's complicated to explain, but basically it works like this: because I am partly deaf, my brain doesn't get all the sounds it needs to be a joyful brain. In turn, my brain makes up its own sounds, which in my case is music that I "hear" in a vague, far-off fashion. It's weird, but I can partially overcome it by keeping my ears occupied. So, I sing to myself.

Most people with MES hear hymns. I fit the description perfectly. I hear "The Old Rugged Cross," "Just as I Am Without One Plea," "I Come to the Garden

Alone," and the one that became Cora's favorite and my great hit song, "Amazing Grace." Although Cora listened politely to the other tunes, "Amazing Grace" was a hit because it touched her heart. I partly hummed it, partly crooned it, and partly whispered to her as we shared the big old sofa. Cora immediately responded to its comforting words and music. Within the first few bars, I felt her tension slipping away until her hesitant little body yielded to the tune, and she crumpled completely down into the folds of her pink pashmina shawl.

Following my "concert," I continued to whisper my love to her as I stroked her head and shoulders. Her response was a gentle, throbbing purr, and then, as I stroked her chin, she stretched out her neck with that "Oh-how-I-love-that!" look on her face. And oh, how that look comforted me. It assured me at least for a short time that Cora's fears and confusion were overcome by contentment and love, which I believe was God's mission for me. So, for me, too, there was "Amazing Grace."

I have one "Amazing Grace" story that I recall with a chuckle. As I drove Cora home from the vet clinic one day, I opened both car windows because it was such a beautiful day. Cora, still groggy from the gabapentin, was in her carrier in the passenger seat. Halfway home she awakened enough to yowl and try to get up. With her movements, the carrier budged an inch or two on the seat. If Cora didn't calm down, things could get risky. My left hand gripped the steering wheel tightly while my right hand fumbled to partly unzip the carrier's top flap. I slipped my hand in to stroke Cora's head to calm her. But my hand might as well have been an annoying flea. Cora shook her head and continued to yowl.

And so, I yowled back at her. But my yowl was "Amazing Grace" at top volume.

The familiar old tune took Cora by surprise. She shut her mouth, and my fingertips felt her tension relax a bit. Encouraged, I kept singing with vigor. The old hymn worked its magic. Cora slumped down in her carrier to relax and listen. I was able to grasp the steering wheel with both hands. The danger was over, but I kept belting out the first verse to the tune over and over, although I suspected Cora would have preferred more variety.

I was having so much fun with a contented cat— the wind in my face and the song in my heart—that I kept on singing even at the stoplight when the teenager in the next car waved and laughed at this crazy old lady who couldn't carry a tune. Really? And who couldn't care less? For Cora and me, "Amazing Grace" became "Our Song"…

Chapter 16

Cora was a master at looking woeful. One quiet night in the fall during the COVID-19 pandemic, she was in her most deplorable state. She lay hunched and pathetic in the middle of the living room floor. Perhaps she was sleepy and content, but to me, she looked forlorn and lonely. When I spoke quietly to her in my poor-dear-little-Cora voice, she hunched herself more tightly which may have signaled she was in her Garbo mood and wished to be alone. However, I interpreted it as poor-little-me-I'm-all-alone. Taking a chance without my armor, I lifted her up to plop her on the sofa. Amazing. Not a squawk, not a hiss, not a muscle moved. Just dead weight.

I sat next to her and eased her onto my lap—still cautious since I'd ditched the heavy leather gloves I'd used to protect myself. As I pulled a small cushion next to my thigh to help ease her weight on me, without opening her eyes, she slowly inched closely to my body. As I watched I held my breath. She tucked her chin between my arm and my chest and wriggled a bit until she was settled into a warm, furry circle in my lap. With two fingers, I delicately stroked small circles between her ears. She didn't move. Slowly I slid those fingers down both sides of her neck—and felt the throbbing of a small purr. Oh my! I sensed we were on the edge of that special kind of communication between a human and an animal that is rare, mystical, and utterly breathtaking.

At that moment, a plane took off from the nearby airport. As its muted throb faded into the night, I realized the room was as silent as snow. Total silence—not even a murmur from the refrigerator or air-conditioning.

I hardly noticed that I began to sing hymns in whispery tones, the ones that seem to relax Cora: "Amazing Grace," "Just as I am Without One Plea," "I Come to the Garden Alone," "Rock of Ages," and "Nearer My God to Thee." As I quietly sang and stroked the circle of fur in my lap, I felt soft and peaceful. The room seemed to enfold us in that small circle in the middle of the sofa. I imagined us as one of those small, round religious paintings in simple frames. I was intensely, yet calmly, aware of God's presence. It was exactly as I had felt the day He gave Cora to me. I smiled as I recalled our COVID Pod: Cora, me, and God.

Cora continued to purr. . .

Chapter 17

One morning, about a year after Cora entered my life, I awakened to find a large urine-yellow puddle on the hardwood floor of the living room. Just beyond it, Cora cowered under a chair staring at it. She raised her eyes to me, and the guilt and embarrassment on her face said it all. I could almost hear her, "It was an accident. I couldn't move fast enough. I'm sorry."

Although I wanted to swoop her up and forgive her, I decided to be casual about it so as not to deepen her embarrassment. I called "good morning" as I dropped the sports section of *The Washington Post* over the puddle and turned to make coffee as if nothing had happened.

I was pleased when Cora joined me in the kitchen and acted as if nothing had happened. Co-conspirators, the two of us bonded in mutual understanding. She didn't pee. I didn't see it. However, the incident nagged me. I tried to put myself in Cora's paws. I imagined a sudden feeling of a desperate bladder, of hoisting myself up and trying to get to the litter box in time. And failing. Every feline instinct must have jarred Cora's natural tendency for cleanliness. No wonder she had looked as if facing The Grand Inquisition. As I silently empathized with her to the point of tears, I was grateful I hadn't been thoughtless enough to shout, "Bad Girl!"

Another morning, a week later, I awakened to find Cora sitting, as still as stone, staring at the wall five inches from her face. She didn't hear me come up behind her. She didn't twitch a whisker when I leaned over and called her name in her ear. She was zoned out. As I've said, this was one kooky cat. I watched this little statue as I ate breakfast and read *The Washington Post*.

I had just reached the comics when Cora turned, shook a back paw, and walked toward her water bowl. I was about to cheer when I noticed something strange; instead of crossing the kitchen straight to the bowl in her bathroom, Cora took the long way by walking close to the wall as if she were blind and needed guidance.

In the following weeks, I noticed that, whenever possible, Cora walked close to the wall. If furniture got in her way she wandered aimlessly as if she were lost. At times she plodded in circles round and round the living room. I watched her with a heavy heart. Finally,

I turned to the Internet to learn Cora most likely was experiencing Cognitive Decline—the beginning of dementia.

Dementia in cats? Who knew? I discovered it was common in older cats. I was amazed to learn 50% of cats who were older than ten years had some degree of dementia due to brain damage or disease. Dementia is a progressive disease with no cure. As I sat at the computer night after night trying to understand what was happening to Cora, I wept. I remembered my husband who had dementia. My emotions were pummeled all over again as I recalled how he clutched his head in his hands and cried out, "What's happening to my brain? Help me, please." I could only imagine what anxiety and pain Cora might be feeling, but, unlike Ward, she had no way of telling me except by roaming around the apartment, obviously very confused.

My research led me to one of the most horrific signs of cat dementia—cats become trapped in corners. They lose the ability to back out of small spaces. I had to rescue Cora four times when she tucked her head into the space between my lounge chair and nightstand. One or two backward steps would have freed her easily, but instead she whimpered until I rescued her. By then, she trusted me implicitly, so after each rescue—without armor—I enfolded her in her pink pashmina shawl and snuggled with her repeating over and over how much I loved her. This was my way of calming the anxiety of dementia instead of following professional advice to stimulate cats with toys and games. At her age, and with her achy joints, Cora had absolutely no interest in cat toys, even those enriched with catnip. Hugs and kisses were my unprofessional remedies.

Cora's most distressing experience of being trapped in a corner happened when I wasn't home. The instant I opened the door on my return, I was paralyzed by ear-splitting cat screams. I dropped my packages and raced through the apartment crying out Cora's name over and over. Panic stricken, I checked all her favorite spots, sobbing, crying "Cora, Cora." And the screaming-yowling grew more desperate.

Finally, I found her, crammed in the two-inch space between the wall and the open bathroom door. She had nosed her way between the door and wall and pushed her body all the way forward. I could see her in the narrow crack between the wall and the door. Her tiny face was terror crazed. Yet, when I pushed the door aside so she could walk out she seemed unfazed. Not even a thank you. She simply walked to her sunny corner window.

I was exhausted as well as an emotional mess. I threw myself on the sofa and bawled like a baby. How long had that poor little terrified cat been stuck? What did she feel like, being totally helpless? I couldn't bear the thought. In those moments, I had my first inkling it might be time to consider putting Cora to sleep. Her quality of life was practically at zero.

Long days and nights of indecision were ahead of me . . .

Chapter 18

Do pets go to heaven? This question hovered in the back of my mind through long days and nights as I weighed the pros and cons of euthanizing Cora. Or, as a gentler way of saying it, "putting her to sleep."

Perhaps the possibility of Cora going to heaven should not have been a consideration of whether to "put her to sleep." The decision should have been based solely on Cora's health and quality of life. I recognized that, but there was always a whisper in my heart telling me my decision would be firmer if I could visualize Cora in heaven agog with youthful curiosity: chasing butterflies, charging in and out of paper bags, and happily exploring heaven's nooks and crannies.

Almost everyone I asked about pets in heaven briefly considered the question, then said yes— they were pretty sure that pets go to heaven. One friend who recently put her dog to sleep didn't hesitate. "Of course," she declared. "Otherwise, it wouldn't be heaven." Her solid, forthright reply grounded my feelings along with some heartening biblical and literary research. I especially liked Billy Graham's answer that "God will provide us with everything we need to be happy in heaven, and if animals are necessary to make us completely happy there you can be confident, He will arrange for them to be with us." Thus, I was comforted by the words of several biblical scholars. Although the Bible doesn't say that animals have eternal life, it implies that they do in passages that describe God's plan to restore his creation; and, of course, animals are part of that creation.

I also searched the Internet for answers. I chuckled at one online comment which asked, "How can these little angels not go to heaven? After their chores are done here, they return to heaven and wait for us." I visualized all these trusty pets, large and small, sitting and waiting, their tongues happily flapping and tails wagging.

Why did I even bother with this question? I knew, deep in my soul, as sure as the sky was blue, that Cora would go to heaven. She was one of God's treasured creatures. He would not desert her. She had been shuffled through an animal shelter and four homes. My apartment was to be her "Forever Home," but an

"Eternal Home" awaited her.

One day I sat on a low chair next to her sunny window haven and idly stroked her back with my stockinged toe. At my touch she stretched slowly and luxuriously, arching her back and sending me a sleepy little sigh of security. "More. More," I could imagine her begging. I then heard a tiny chirping sound. It was coming from Cora's mouth which was quivering in anticipation of delight the way that cats chatter when they spot a nearby bird.

I dug my toe deeper into the thick fur of her ruff. With one last chirp, Cora melted her body into a circle of fluffy fur. Both paws were raised. One settled like a pussy willow bud under her chin, the other curled languidly over her left eye. Sound asleep.

I did what I often do. I cried a little. I admit it— I'm a crier. Tears flood me easily for both joy and sorrow. And Cora offered excellent opportunities for both. If for nothing else, by bringing joy, beauty, love, and a smidgen of kookiness to my life, Cora irrefutably deserved a place in heaven…

Chapter 19

"When it is time to euthanize Cora, that responsibility is part of your loving duty to her." This short, wise, and powerful advice from my cat-loving friend, Bob, held me steadfast when I finally reached the decision that my God-given mission to Cora was to euthanize her. In addition to all the signs of her diminished quality of life such as walking in circles, staring at blank walls, and getting trapped in corners, Cora totally lacked energy. The ultimate decision came when, for three nights in a row, she hunched herself in the most inaccessible spot in the apartment as animals do in the wild when they are ready to die.

Her vet agreed it was time. I wanted it done at home to save Cora from the trauma of gabapentin and her hated carrier. I wanted her last moments to be as comfortable and peaceful as possible. Her veterinarian did not provide home euthanasia, but she recommended a group of vets called Laps of Love that specialized in it. I was pleased to learn my rector had used Laps of

Love to euthanize her dog and recommended them highly. She also told me that parishioners' pets could be buried in the church's St. Francis Garden next to a small stone statue of the saint. Moreover, I learned that our Episcopal church had a short liturgy especially for animals. My mood lightened; everything I learned supported my difficult decision.

Everything went smoothly, quickly, and efficiently. I was able to get an appointment the following morning. The veterinarian who came to my apartment was a major "cat person" who at one time owned seven cats all at once. I had snuggled Cora into her pink pashmina shawl. The doctor and I chatted briefly as both of us stroked Cora, then she allowed me a brief time to whisper my goodbyes in Cora's ears and kiss her sweet forehead in farewell before she administered two quick shots that put Cora peacefully to sleep forever. It seemed to happen in the blink of an eye. Swiftly and gently, the doctor placed Cora in a lined wicker basket, then covered her to her shoulders with a fluffy blue towel. I thanked God she looked completely at peace.

The doctor left with a parting reminder that Cora's ashes would be returned by mail from the out-of-town crematorium. She complimented me on how calm and controlled I was. I didn't consider it a compliment. It made me sound cold and uncaring. In fact, I was speechless and overwhelmed. I remember sitting down, dry-eyed and staring into space for a long time.

I had little time to mourn Cora because a few hours later I was hit hard with a gastrointestinal disease that suddenly rampaged through our building. For twenty-four hours I was violently ill, followed by another thirty-six hours of dead-to-the-world sleep; so almost three days passed after Cora was taken to the crematory before it finally hit me that she was gone. I howled. I sank into grief. I was desperate. My heart ached. Oh God, how I missed her! The pain of losing Cora was so strong, I felt it physically. I threw myself onto the sofa and buried my head in the folds of the pink pashmina shawl that was still bunched in the corner. I remembered how I had flung myself onto Ward's bed when he died and cried and cried into his pillow.

Since those first agonizing days, I have been somewhat consoled by beautiful memories. One of the most powerful and vivid is of the two of us snuggling on the sofa every night while I watched the news and Cora snoozed in her shawl. I recall how she stretched out her neck in utter sensual delight when I stroked her delicate chin with its little white muzzle. Her eyes were closed. There was almost a smile on her face as if she were already in heaven. Watching that contented little creature, I was overcome with tenderness and love. Many times, in those quiet moments, I leaned over to kiss her forehead and whisper how much I loved her.

As I write this, two months have passed. The physical pain has mostly healed, but the heaviness in my heart remains. There is a tiny, sudden, heartache each time I return to the apartment and there is no one, not Ward or Cora, to greet me nor anyone to kiss goodnight when I go to bed.

One thought that saddens me is that I never saw Cora in her kittenhood and youth. I never saw her tumbling and stalking a crumpled paper ball or a fuzzy-felt mouse. As a supporter of Hope for Paws, a wonderful animal life-saving organization, I watch its videos of kittens who have been saved from tragic circumstances. I get teary eyed as I watch those tiny angels, restored to health, happily tumble, and cavort. Was Cora ever this agile? This fun-filled? Has she returned to that state in heaven?

I'm amazed at how many people have euthanized a pet at some time in their lives, and how they become tearful when we talk about it even many years later. It's a sad topic, but also a hopeful one because most of these pet owners expect to be reunited somehow, someday. The day after Cora died, a friend slipped a sympathy note under my door along with a comforting poem entitled "The Ridge." It was written about sixty years ago by a teen-age girl named Carol Notermann, whose cat had died. She poured her young heart and soul into it. The lines that give me goosebumps describe how her cat has been playing in a heavenly place for many years, but one day she sees a person, her owner, coming up the hill toward her. "IT'S YOU! IT'S YOU! It's really you! You've come to be with me!" the cat cries as the two embrace and cover one another with kisses. I hope to hear Cora call that out to me someday.

Since then, I'm comforting myself with Cora's precious pink pashmina shawl. I wrap myself in it every night as I curl up on our big old sofa to watch the news. As I snuggle into its lightweight warmth, I'm flooded with beautiful memories of Cora's heart-shaped face peeking from its folds. That's when I scrunch down and shed a tear . . . yet another tear in tribute to the world's most adored cat…

Chapter 20

For months after I kissed Cora goodbye, I continued to have sudden outbursts of crying. I was unusually tired. I said to myself: "You believe Cora is in heaven, so why cry? You should feel joyful, or at least content and comforted." Still, I was heartbroken by an image of Cora that haunted me every day.

I vividly relived the days when I returned home after being away for a while. Cora would painfully rise to her feet and slowly come to me on wobbly legs. She would stop at my feet and simply stand there, not moving, with her head hanging down. "Oh, you poor little penitent" I cried playfully. "Are you asking forgiveness from a Supreme Ancient Goddess?"

She looked so pitiful that I couldn't resist her. So, of course, each time I leaned over and called her name loudly to give her the attention she wanted. I was as delighted as she was as I ruffled the fur around her neck and between her ears; then slipped my fingers down to her chest to lightly massage it; and moving further downward, cupped and kneaded the rounded muscles of her upper foreleg in my palms. Each time, my fingertips discovered the delicate throb of a soft purr.

It was a beautiful moment, but it was much more than that because each time I understood instantly it was the golden key in our relationship. Hence, I treasure it. As Cora's dementia deepened and she was confused by everything around her, I gradually realized she came to me because I was the one thing she recognized. My touch grounded her. It offered security and a sense of belonging despite her muddled mind. Even now, the mere thought of those moments together breaks my heart. I weep for those times when that sweet little cat needed me, came to me, and the two of us comforted one another with compassion, pity, love, and warmth. I thank God daily for His gift to me—the gift of being able to offer that mutely pleading tiny body both the love and security she needed and deserved.

Nevertheless, no matter how much it comforted me to recall how I helped Cora, my thoughts clung to memories of her neediness. Through prayer and a lot of late-night reflection, I gradually realized I was letting myself be overwhelmed by memories of Cora's needs, confusion, and physical pain; in turn, it tore me up. I couldn't shake the image of her at my feet with her head bowed in a silent request for a loving touch. That gesture will remain in my heart forever where I will treasure it. However, common sense and answers to prayers told me that I must shift my thoughts to more positive aspects of my life with Cora. I tried to recall how I had helped her, how often I kissed her, and whispered in her ear how much I loved her. Surely God gave her the sensitivity to understand my actions and words. I imagined how warm she must have felt, literally, nestled next to me in her pink shawl. I imagined how she must have felt, spiritually, in the warmth of my kisses and whispered words of love. Although I will always yearn to hold my lovely Cora again, my heartache has gradually eased as I have focused on the security and comfort in which I enfolded her and not on her neediness and confusion.

Many people ask if I plan to get another cat. I know they mean well, but do they think a cat is like a coffee cup? Break one, get another? Here's the truth of the matter: Cora is irreplaceable. Although I mourn my beautiful Cora every day, with God's help I know and accept His will for both of us has been done. She lifted my spirits; she gave me a purpose to live, love, and enjoy life again. My loving care brought her back to life for many tender months together and I believe it soothed her anxieties as her mind and body declined. She had been on a joyful loan to me. Now, Cora has returned to God—of this I am certain. I am also sure that one day God, Cora, and I, along with cat-loving Ward, five Siamese, and one Himalayan will be a pod once again.

The End

With appreciation for the IT skills of Victor Otusanya.

Printed in the USA
CPSIA information can be obtained
at www.ICGtesting.com
JSHW021934170823
46759JS00001B/55